Global Issues

Project Organizer

2

Series Editor
Barclay Lelievre
Mike East

Name:

 OXFORD
UNIVERSITY PRESS

T0320784

Great Clarendon Street, Oxford OX2 6DP

Oxford University Press is a department of the University of Oxford.
It furthers the University's objective of excellence in research, scholarship,
and education by publishing worldwide in

Oxford   New York

Auckland   Cape Town   Dar es Salaam   Hong Kong   Karachi
Kuala Lumpur   Madrid   Melbourne   Mexico City   Nairobi
New Delhi   Shanghai   Taipei   Toronto

With offices in

Argentina   Austria   Brazil   Chile   Czech Republic   France   Greece
Guatemala   Hungary   Italy   Japan   Poland   Portugal   Singapore
South Korea   Switzerland   Thailand   Turkey   Ukraine   Vietnam

© Oxford University Press

The moral rights of the authors have been asserted

Database right Oxford University Press (maker)

First published 2009

British Library Cataloguing in Publication Data

Data available

ISBN: 978-0-19-918080-6

10 9 8 7

Printed in Great Britain by Ashford Colour Press Ltd., Gosport.

Paper used in the production of this book is a natural, recyclable product made
from wood grown in sustainable forests. The manufacturing process conforms to
the environmental regulations to the country of origin.

Author acknowledgments
To Avery, Eve, and Hayden for their patience and for sharing their Dad for a year.
Barclay Lelievre

Thank you to my family and the Colegio Internacional de Caracas for the
unwavering support you have given me. *Mike East*

The publishers would like to thank Talei Kunkel and Lisa Nicholson for their advice,
and the International Baccalaureate and Anita Knight, Isabel Machinandiarena,
Patrick Sweeney, and Annie Termaat for permission to reproduce the learner profile
on page 5 which originally appeared in *MYP Interact* (International Baccalaureate,
2008).

Companion website:
www.OxfordSecondary.co.uk/myp

Contents

Introduction

This is the second of five Project Organizers which focus on interdisciplinary learning, in this case having an overarching theme of agriculture. The series reflects key aspects of the philosophy and approach of the IB Middle Years Programme, including: being internationally minded, demonstrating academic honesty, and developing the qualities of the IB learner profile:

Interdisciplinary learning

Most often in school you will be timetabled to study different subjects at different times. In life you will be mixing the skills and knowledge from these different subjects to understand things and solve problems. The projects in this book encourage you to use more than one subject to approach the unit questions. The first page of each unit shows the unit question and the two or more focus subjects.

International-mindedness

Today's students need to explore a blend of the local, the national and the international. We only have one planet and the way we act affects it and all life upon it. The chapters in this book will show the links between us and people and places all over the world.

Academic honesty

We all want others to think highly of us. Academic honesty is a set of values and skills that promote personal integrity when doing exams, assignments and homework. By following these values and skills we demonstrate that we are honest and principled.

The IB learner profile

The International Baccalaureate aims to develop internationally minded people who, recognizing their common humanity and shared guardianship of the planet, help to create a better and more peaceful world. IB learners strive to be:

Inquirers
You are curious and ask important questions to inquire into the world around you. You research independently and love learning throughout life.

Knowledgeable
Through your keen exploration of local and global issues you build an in-depth knowledge and understanding across all subject areas.

Thinkers
You think both critically and creatively to help solve problems and make responsible decisions.

Communicators
You are able to understand and express yourself confidently in more than one language. You work well and enthusiastically in team situations.

Principled
You demonstrate honesty, a sense of fairness and respect towards those around you. You take responsibility for your own actions.

Open-minded
You take pride in who you are. You are respectful of others' opinions, traditions and values. You consider more than one point of view when making decisions.

Caring
You are considerate towards the needs of others. You are committed to making a positive difference to others and to the environments.

Risk-takers
You are confident and show courage in new situations. You are keen to try new things. You defend your own beliefs strongly.

Balanced
You recognize the importance of caring for yourself, balancing your physical, emotional and intellectual self (all parts of you!).

Reflective
You think carefully about how you learn through different experiences. By being able to recognize your strengths and limitations you can set goals for further learning and development.

How to use this book

This book is to help inspire and structure interdisciplinary work on global themes. You will gradually populate and personalize your Project Organizer throughout the year, with the completed organizer acting as a record of your interdisciplinary work, along with the folders and other pieces of work that you build up. We hope that you enjoy the units and the challenges that they present!

1 Poverty and hunger

Unit question
How can what I eat now mean less for me later?

Subject focus and objectives

Mathematics
Knowledge and understanding
- Can you use appropriate mathematical concepts and skills to solve simple problems in a real-life context?

Communication in mathematics
- Can you use different forms of mathematical representation (tables and graphs)?

Reflection in mathematics
- Can you consider the importance of your findings?

Technology
Investigate
- Can you collect and select information and organize it logically?

Plan
- Can you construct a plan to create the product that makes effective use of your resources?

Create
- Can you follow the plan to make the product with minimal guidance?

Evaluate
- Can you reconsider the success of the program, based on its use and your own views?

Area of interaction
Community and service
- This unit considers taking action to reduce our carbon footprint.

Approaches to learning focus
Communication
- Informing others using a variety of media.

Information literacy
- Selecting and organizing information, making connections between resources.

Starting points

Why is farming so important?

For city people in the developed world, most food comes from a supermarket and water from a tap. As we go about our daily lives, the decisions taken to get food into our shops seem to be the concern of others. It is easy to forget just how closely our well-being depends on our relationship with the land.

Agricultural choices

Here are some decisions that a commercial farmer has to make:

What should I farm?

- Is it best to raise animals and/or crops?
- Should I farm for food or for industrial purposes?

Should fertilizers be used?

- They increase the yield by adding nitrates to the soil, but can damage the environment if the nitrates wash into rivers.
- Is there a natural alternative available?

Should pesticides be used?

- They increase the yield, but can enter the food cycle and poison other creatures, including humans.
- Could a natural predator eat the pest threatening the crop?

Reflection

Is there any way you, as a consumer, can influence farmers' decisions?

_____

_____

Some facts about farming

- Over 33% of the world's people get their main income from farming.
- Agriculture covers 33% of the Earth's land surface.
- 96% of farmers live in developing countries.
- About 75% of the workforce in the Least Developed Countries farm.
- 25% of all the farmers in the world live in India.
- 70% of the fresh water consumed in human activity is used in agriculture.
- Just 30 different crop varieties make up about 80% of the food we eat.

How does your lifestyle affect the environment?

1. Use the following website to calculate your carbon footprint from your diet: http://www.eatlowcarbon.org/

2. Discuss your result with your classmates.

3. What similarities and differences are there in the class?

_____

_____

_____

4. How did what you eat increase or decrease your carbon footprint?

_____

_____

Reflection

Read the red box and page 74. If the demand for meat continues to increase, what impact will it have on:

a global warming?

_____

_____

b the grain needed to support meat production?

_____

_____

You have just looked at how your own lifestyle impacts on agriculture and the environment. The next page describes some global trends that are threatening to create a future world with increased poverty and hunger.

Some food statistics

- Producing half a kilogram of beef generates 13 times more greenhouse gasses than producing half a kilogram of chicken, and 57 times more than producing half a kilogram of potatoes.

- For every 2.8 kilograms of food the cow eats, 30% is lost as heat in respiration and 60% in urine and faeces. Only 10% is converted into the cow's growth. In other words, a cow is 90% inefficient!

- Of the 36 billion tons of greenhouse gases we produce each year, 18% comes from meat production. Only energy generation contributes more.

- Four billion people now want to add more meat to their diets, especially in rapidly developing countries like China and India.

Agriculture and the future

All of the following trends are putting stresses on the agricultural system:

⇨ Each year roughly another 70 million people are added to the global population. This means that enough extra food has to be found – every year – to feed more than the entire population of France, and more than double the population of Canada.

⇨ With the development of biofuels, enough US grain to feed a billion people in the developing world is now being converted into car fuel instead (see Unit 5).

⇨ Underground water is being pumped out faster than it can be replaced naturally (much of it for agricultural use). In India, 175 million people rely on irrigation from wells that will soon be exhausted.

⇨ Soil is eroding and being lost faster than new soil is forming.

⇨ Valuable farmland is disappearing under concrete as cities expand.

⇨ As global warming continues, each 1 degree centigrade (1.8 degrees Fahrenheit) rise above normal temperatures reduces wheat, corn and rice yields by 10%.

⇨ Rising costs are forcing farmers to borrow more money to buy seeds and pesticides, increasing their debt load.

The increasing demand for water in agriculture to feed the growing global population is putting a strain on water reserves, like the dried up river above. Both photos are from India.

What is permaculture?

Some farming methods involve working the land until it is exhausted. Permaculture is a system where the ecosystem renews itself and continues to produce high yields. It focuses on using local knowledge of the land, the soil and species that will thrive there. The principle is to take the minimum amount of land necessary for cultivation, and leave the rest as a biodiversity reserve for plants and animals. Permaculture involves observation and reflection before action.

There are three guiding principles for permaculture:

⟶ **Earth care** includes the belief that we are part of the Earth, not separate from it. Natural resources are not used any faster than nature renews them, and people work with natural systems instead of against them. Waste is cut down to a minimum and recycled.

⟶ **People care** is a philosophy where the community works together and the needs of its different members are considered. As much as possible is made locally.

⟶ **Fair shares** blends earth care and people care together to ensure that people today have access to what they need, as well as future generations and other species (also called sustainability).

Critics say that permaculture needs to prove statistically that it can do all the things its supporters claim of it.

Reflection

1   What are the strengths and weaknesses of permaculture?

_____

_____

2   How can permaculture really help to solve the current problems in agriculture, which are threatening to create a future world of poverty and hunger?

_____

_____

_____

_____

Population growth

In this activity you will work out an arithmetic sequence to approximate global population growth.

1 The horizontal axis on the graph below covers the years 1998 to 2025.

2 Plot two pieces of data on your vertical axis. The first is global population. According to Lester Brown, an environmental expert, global population is increasing at more than 70 million people a year. However, because population growth is now levelling out, you will plot the increase arithmetically at 70 million a year.

   → If you are doing this exercise in 2010, start with a total global population of 6,800,000,000 and add 70 million people for each year up to 2025. Work out the arithmetic sequence on notepaper. Add it to the graph when your teacher has checked your work.

   → If you are doing this exercise in another year, find out the current global population total and start from that. Add 70 million people for each year up to 2025.

   → In addition, find out the global population totals for previous years and add them to the graph. Go back as far as 1998.

3 Also on the vertical axis, plot the global grain reserves (in days) available in each year from the table on the right.

4 After you have plotted the global grain reserves, join them up with a line and observe the trend. Continue the line as best you can up to the year 2025.

5 Consider the importance of your findings. Discuss them with your classmates and relate them to other issues discussed in this chapter.

> An **arithmetic sequence** increases or decreases at a constant rate. The numbers in this sequence are called **terms**.
>
> To find the next term in an arithmetic sequence, take the previous term (a) and add the difference to it (d). For example, a sequence could be shown as:
> a1, a1 + d, a1 + 2d, a1 + 3d, a1 + 4d ... etc.
>
> If the term is 20 and the increase is 4, the arithmetic sequence would be:
> 20, 24, 28, 32, 36 ... etc.

Year	Global grain reserves (in days)
1998	115
1999	115
2000	111
2001	102
2002	84
2003	67
2004	74
2005	71
2006	61
2007	55

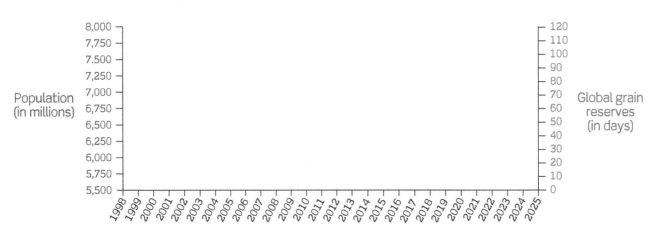

Our project plan

For this activity, you are going to use a computer program to create a presentation that will use a combination of images, sounds and text. One program that does this is called Photo Story. Your teacher will decide if you will use this or a similar program and set up the resources accordingly.

The question you will be answering is:

What are the human and environmental pressures on our agricultural system?

Use information from this unit and elsewhere in this Project Organizer to help you, particularly from Unit 6.

You should complete this task by following the steps of the design cycle below:

Investigate
Step 1: With the above question in mind, look through the information available in this Project Organizer and add research of your own.

Step 2: There is much information available. Select the most important.

Plan

Step 1: Sketch out your ideas on a planner like the one below. You will need many (perhaps 12-20) slides to complete the task, so you should copy and repeat this planner as many times as necessary in order to organize your ideas completely.

Step 2: Reference your sources.

Step 3: When your plan is ready, show it to your teacher for approval before you begin the detailed work.

Example slide planner

Which photo or image will I use? Describe the effects you will combine with it.

_____

_____

_____

Text to accompany this image:

_____

_____

_____

_____

_____

Sound/music/voice over effect:

_____

Remember
A piece of work like this will draw on many resources, so you will need to reference both your images and your text using a system that your teacher will give you.

Create

Step 1: Open the program and follow the plan.

Step 2: Present your work to your classmates.

Step 3: Listen to the feedback and make any changes you wish.

Step 4: Give the work to your teacher.

Evaluate

Step 1: Consider the strengths and weaknesses of this program. Did it allow you to create the product you wanted?

Step 2: Consider how your product itself could be improved.

Taking action

Talking about global issues can sometimes lead to doom and gloom, because some of the problems are so large. It is often better to focus on solutions. As you are the future decision makers, how will you make your world a better place?

Have you considered making your school greener - something you could perhaps do through your student council/leadership? In this case, you could take any of the ideas you like to your teachers and administrators. Similarly, have you thought of making changes at home and getting your family involved?

Any or all of these things could make great **Community and service** projects:

Permaculture – on a small scale.
Could you take part of the school grounds and/or a garden and grow your own food using the principles of permaculture?

Water – is an increasingly valuable resource.
Put large plastic barrels under the pipes that drain the rainwater from the roof. After the rainwater has collected in your barrel, you could use buckets of it to water your permaculture garden.

Windowsills and balconies – are places where you can also grow things.
How about some herbs, chillies or salad vegetables?

Biodiversity – much of which is being lost because of modern farming methods.
Investigate how diverse the wildlife is around your school. Dedicate part of the school grounds as a reserve. Study the animals and plants that live there.

School food – How healthy is the food in your school?
Where does the food come from? Could the suppliers purchase fresher food grown locally? Investigate.

School waste – Where does the organic waste from the school canteen go?
Could it be used to make compost for your permaculture garden?

Health – has a big effect on educational achievement.
Carry out a survey on health and diet issues in the school.

And from there, you could move on to preserving the Earth's resources:

Recycling – Many schools are doing this already, but are you doing it to its fullest extent – paper, aluminium, plastic, glass, unwanted clothes? What else could you include?

A sun station – Place solar panels on the roof. Many of these are guaranteed to last 20 years.

Solar roof tiles – These generally last over 50 years and can generate so much energy for a house that you can even make a profit from it if you live in a place where you can sell your excess energy back to the energy supplier. This is true even in countries with notoriously bad weather, such as Britain.

Investigate these ideas on the Internet: **Solar4schools, the Green Schools Initiative, eco-schools**

Some of these initiatives are quite new and the technology is changing all the time. You could become world leaders in these kinds of projects.

BUT remember that there is usually lots of enthusiasm at the beginning. How will you maintain your project in the long term?

Reflection

Try to link each of the suggestions above to the problems mentioned in this unit. Which suggestions, do you think, would be the most effective in helping to relieve these problems? Why? What other suggestions could you make? Discuss your thoughts with your classmates.

Project evaluation

What I enjoyed about this unit, and why

_____

_____

What aspect I didn't enjoy, and why

_____

_____

What I did really well

_____

_____

What I did less well

_____

_____

What I would do differently next time

_____

_____

_____

Which project work I liked best, and why

_____

_____

_____

Moving on

Problems

1 Thomas Malthus had different ideas about population growth and food supply. They are linked to the arithmetic sequencing exercise that you completed earlier. Find out about them.

2 Investigate what a failed or failing state is.

- Which countries are in most danger of becoming failed states?
- What are the dangers of living in a failed state?
- What are the dangers to other countries?
- What are the indicators of a failing state?
- How can states be helped to avoid failing?
- How do failing states recover?

Solutions

3 Investigate initiatives that encourage people to eat in a more sustainable way, such as the Local Food Movement, also known as locavores, and the 100-mile diet. Do you have one in your area? Find out what the advantages and disadvantages of this type of initiative are.

A farmers' market in Britain - the food has to be produced within 30 miles of the market for it to be officially certified

4 Find out about the term 'food sovereignty' and the principles behind it. Do you think that these ideas could help to avoid a future of poverty and hunger for many?

2 Conflict and peace

Unit question

How can we learn from the mistakes of the past?

Subject focus and objectives

Humanities
Change

- Can you provide some explanations for links between causes and consequences?
- Can you understand that changes occur when people interact with their environment?

Language A
Content

- Can you compose a scene from a screenplay that tells the story of a collapsing society?

Organization

- Can you use the rules of script writing?

Music
Knowledge and understanding

- Can you describe features of soundtracks/soundscapes that make them effective?

Application

- Can you create a soundscape/soundtrack for a scene in a movie?

Area of interaction
Human ingenuity

- Humans can create problems when they transform the landscape around them. Can we learn from civilizations that failed to find solutions to their problems?

Approaches to learning focus
Thinking

- Combining creative and critical strategies to consider the consequences of agricultural/resource mismanagement.

The mysterious statues of Easter Island

EXT. DAY. DECK OF A MERCHANT SHIP.

SUPER: A TERRIBLE STORM HAS BLOWN A GERMAN MERCHANT SHIP FROM THE INHOSPITABLE WATERS OF THE GREENLAND SEA INTO AN UNCHARTED FJORD.

A rugged sailor, KAPITAN JON SCHIFFER, stands beside his pilot as he surveys the shore for a place to put in.

MIDSHIPMAN:
Kapitan! A village! On the south shore!

All eyes turn to see a series of half-ruined buildings in the distance, overgrown with tough grass and in disrepair.

KAPITAN JON:
Ready a party to go ashore!

The cold sun does nothing to warm the hands of the sailors as they quietly row.

SAILOR #1:
Kapitan! I saw something moving.

KAPITAN JON:
Steady boys. Swords ready.

As they come ashore they discover the source of the motion; a haggard looking wild ram. A figure lies face down in front of a building. A strange woollen hood covers the head and the clothing is made of sealskin. A curved and well-worn knife lies beside him. The party approaches.

MIDSHIPMAN:
Hey, Mister! Wake up!

As he rolls the figure over, the party startles. At their feet is a long-dead skeleton.

SAILOR #1:
Who is he Kapitan?

KAPITAN JON:
A Viking. (beat) And, from the looks of it, the last one.

The remains of a Viking church in southern Greenland

The text on the left is an excerpt from a screenplay based on the novel *The Viking Saga* by Peter Brent (Tinling, Prescott, 1975), which tells the tale of the doomed Viking settlement of Greenland between the years 1000 and 1400.

A number of civilizations have collapsed due to the mismanagement of resources, especially food and agriculture. You will look at several examples of this and consider whether the past is in danger of repeating itself, and if we can learn from past mistakes to avoid it happening again.

From hunter-gatherers to farmers

One of the main theories about why humans moved from being hunter-gatherers to farmers has to do with the destruction of larger prey species such as the woolly mammoth. Whether these animals met their ends due to climate change or over-hunting, humans were left struggling to find a reliable alternative food supply.

Research

2.5 million years ago	Our ancestors began to use tools for hunting
15,000 years ago	Humans had spread around the globe
12,000 years ago	Humans began farming
5,000 years ago	The majority of humans had moved over to farming and the first civilizations had risen in Iraq and Egypt
3,000 years ago	Human civilizations existed in the Americas, Africa, Asia and Europe

> 1   Which species have become extinct in the last 200-300 years?
> 2   Were any of these extinctions related to over-hunting?
>
> You could check the International Union for the Conservation of Nature's 'Red List', to learn more about species in danger of extinction or recent extinctions.
> http://www.iucnredlist.org/

The village on the right in Heshmatabad, Iran, has the same sort of mud-walled, thatch-roofed houses that were around when agriculture began in the area 7,000 years ago. The close quarters and large populations that sometimes accompany a switch from a nomadic way of life to an agricultural, sedentary one would have posed some unique problems for the first farmers.

Settling down

What possible problems could people face by living in settlements that they would probably not have experienced as nomads/hunter-gatherers?

sedentary • adjective • Remaining in one location, not migratory, settled.

Make a list of possible problems on your own. Then get together with a partner and compare your lists. Your teacher will then put you into a larger group to share your ideas.

THINK • PAIR • SHARE

As farming began to develop in many places around the world, humans also began to domesticate and herd animals like llama, goats, sheep and cattle.

In spite of the problems you listed above, agriculture and farming is the number one occupation in the world today, especially in developing countries. It stands to reason that there must be some benefits to it. Repeat the activity above for the question: 'What are some of the benefits of living in a society supported by agriculture?'

Human nature

Before we look at different civilizations and the agricultural systems that sustained them, we really need to consider human nature a little more carefully. What are we *really* like?

In the nineteenth century, many people believed in the idea of civilization moving onwards towards ever-greater progress. As industrialization continued to develop new technology, that idea stayed with us. Are we now more civilized, and more responsible when managing our resources and environment?

Have a look at the table below and fill in your thoughts. When you decide about each answer, remember that someone in your class or in another group will ask you: 'What makes you say that?'. Be sure that you can answer this question.

Human quality	Definition	In your opinion, is this human quality increasing, decreasing or staying the same in your society? Give an example and an explanation to back up your response.
Envy		
Ingenuity		
Greed		
Love		
Violence		
Compassion		
Hatred		
Stewardship		

Look at your completed table and decide whether you think societies are evolving into something 'better'. Are humans becoming more perfect? *What makes you say that?* Discuss with your class.

Now that you have thought a bit more about human nature, this unit will start to consider the connections with agriculture, resources and the unit question in more detail:

How can we learn from the mistakes of the past?

Easter Island: The mystery of Rapa Nui

Easter Island is famous for the huge statues that litter its landscape (see right). The Easter Islanders created these monuments to their ancestors and erected them so that they would look across the lands of their clan. Through hard work, the gently sloping, fertile, volcanic soil was made more productive, and the island's population grew as a result of the increased harvests. This system produced a food surplus that allowed a complex society to evolve. The rulers fed the labourers who created the statues. However, this complex society eventually began to unravel and, after a series of bad decisions about natural resources, the society descended into chaos, warfare, and cannibalism.

Rwanda: A modern day collapse?

In the heart of Africa lies the tiny country of Rwanda. In 1994, many Rwandans turned on each other and about 800,000 (11% of the population) were murdered by their leaders, their neighbors, their workmates, and even their relatives. Why did this slaughter happen? While it is true that extremist politicians exploited historical tensions between the majority Hutus (85% of the population) and the minority Tutsis (15%), it doesn't tell the whole story. There were underlying problems to do with agriculture and access to natural resources, including:

The Easter Island statues are also known as *Moai*

- Rwanda's population density
- the availability of land
- soil erosion
- shrinking farm sizes
- deforestation
- land disputes.

All these factors created more hunger and more desperation and contributed to the crisis.

Rwandan refugees who have fled to a neighboring country receive medical aid in 1994

Anasazi: People of the Pueblos

In the 'four-corner' region of the American Southwest are found the ancient adobe dwellings of a once great society, the Anasazi. Anthropologists put their numbers as high as 4,000 at the civilization's peak. Although they had no formal writing system, their history is reflected in their amazing architecture and other remains. What could have happened to cause the collapse of this society?

The Anasazi settlement at Mesa Verde, Colorado

Somalia: A perfect storm

In the early 1990s, the streets of Mogadishu, Somalia's capital, descended into anarchy. Roving gangs from different clans roamed the city in machine gun-fitted trucks, called 'technicals', opening fire on each other and killing thousands of innocent civilians in the crossfire. Famine raged throughout the country, killing hundreds of thousands of Somalis. International food aid poured in, but much of it went undelivered or was stolen, showing up on the black market at hyper-inflated prices. The situation became so desperate that the United Nations took the unprecedented step of approving the invasion of Somalia by a coalition of troops, largely American, in order to distribute food aid. So, how did it get so bad? How did conflict and agriculture come together to create this 'perfect storm' of chaos?

Somali gunmen from one clan patrolling the streets of Mogadishu in their 'technical', an old truck armed with heavy machine guns

Our project plan

Making predictions

Choose ONE of the societies from the list on the right. Do some research and complete the table below. Focus on the details of the collapse, the consequences of each detail, and the possible solutions which might have prevented/fixed the problem in the first place. Use a separate piece of paper, if necessary. Be sure to include the sources where your information came from.

- Vikings – Greenland
- Polynesians – Easter Island
- Tutsis/Hutus – Rwanda
- Anasazi – New Mexico
- Somalia
- Any other suitable example (please check with your teacher)

Actions/events which contributed to the collapse	Consequences for the society if the problem is not dealt with	Practical solutions to avoid or fix the problem

Making connections

1   Where, in the modern world, might you find examples of some of the problems you identified above?
2   What lessons can be learned today from the mistakes made by the civilization in your research?
3   How many of your findings were related to food/agriculture?

Compare your list of actions/events which led to the collapse of a named society with the class brainstorm.
What are the similarities?

Your teacher will provide you with the rubric to assess the research in the above table and the answers to your connections questions.

Brainstorm

As a class, come up with a list of reasons why humans are reluctant to change their way of life. Why do we continue to repeat the mistakes of the past?

Writing a screenplay

Screenplays, like the one on page 20, are an interesting way to get your message across. There is a set of rules which all screenwriters use. The example below should help to explain some of them:

The scene on the right contains the essential elements of a screenplay:

> The slugline – This tells you where the scene is taking place (INT – interior shot, EXT – exterior shot), the location (in this case a CLASSROOM), and finally the time of day (DAY or NIGHT).

> Action – This describes what is happening on the screen, and which characters (if any) are involved. In this case Shane, his classmates and a teacher. The action is sometimes capitalized for effect.

> Character name – This always appears centred and capitalized.

> Dialogue – This is indented from both sides. It is the words the characters speak. It is never bolded or italicized. Details of the character's speech may be included in brackets, and pauses in speech can be shown by including the instruction (beat), as illustrated on the right.

INT. CLASSROOM – DAY

Shane sits quietly reading in a roomful of students, teacher at her desk. He suddenly SCREAMS, jumping from his seat. Classmates startle.

SHANE:
(to teacher)
I can't believe you are making us do this!
(to class)
Can you believe she is making us do this!

FRANK:
I swear I am going to do it!
(beat)
I swear I'll do it ...
(dissolves into tears)

Activity

Write **one scene** for a movie being made about the collapse of a society, based on the mismanagement of food and resources. It might be an historic collapse, or one set in the not-too-distant future. Be creative!

You could use the information contained in the table you researched earlier, plus the discussions and brainstorming exercise you did in class, to help you with your writing, or you could do some further research.

Your teacher will provide you with the rubric that will be used to assess the piece.

In Egypt's sandy silence, all alone,
Stands a gigantic Leg, which far off throws
The only shadow that the Desert knows:
"I am great OZYMANDIAS," saith the stone,
"The King of Kings; this mighty City shows
"The wonders of my hand." The City's gone,
Nought but the Leg remaining to disclose
The site of this forgotten Babylon.

By Horace Smith

Writing a soundtrack

Now you are going to work on a musical composition/ soundscape which charts the progress of a civilization that started from simple beginnings, rose to greatness, and then fell because of its failure to feed itself and manage its natural resources. Think of it as the soundtrack to the movie you have begun writing.

Before beginning, you might like to find existing music from soundtracks or movie scores. These are available at various websites, or from your music teacher, or you could simply turn away from a movie you are watching and listen to the score for some ideas.

Some questions that you will need to consider in the music you listen to, and the music you compose, are:

- Which instruments/sound effects will I use?
- What kind of chords and chord progressions (if any) will I use?
- How can I create different moods?
- How will I notate or write down the soundscape/ composition. Soundscapes do not require the ability to write music – as long as you create a system that you can read and explain to someone else, so that they can then play it. Three examples are shown on the right and on the next page.

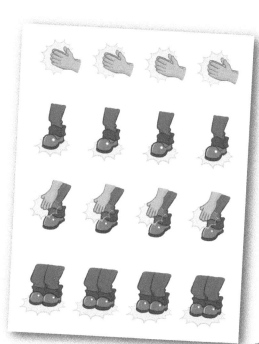

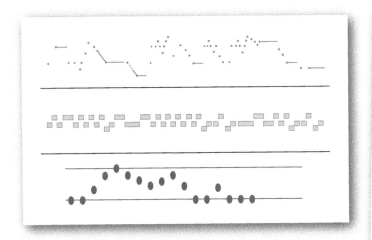

For your composition, you need to consider the following things:

1   The mood of your piece needs to reflect the stages that your chosen civilization actually went through. It should include most, or perhaps all, of the following phases:

  → The farmers plant their crops and harvest them.
  → With time, food is plentiful, the civilization grows – progress.
  → Problems begin; the civilization over-reaches itself.
  → The problems worsen – conflict begins.
  → A disastrous collapse occurs.
  → There is a sense of loss and wonder at what happened.

2   The musical style you choose for the basis of your composition should have some type of link to it – either culturally, geographically or historically – although you should add your own touches as well.

3   Consider the use of sound effects. If you use them, how much should they intrude into the music?

After you have created your initial version of your composition:

  → play it to the class and your teacher
  → see if how they interpret the music is similar to the reaction you intended
  → listen to the feedback, take notes and make any changes
  → present your final work to your teacher.

Your teacher will provide you with the rubric with which your piece will be assessed.

Project evaluation

What I enjoyed about this unit, and why

What aspect I didn't enjoy, and why

What I did really well

What I did less well

What I would do differently next time

Which project work I liked best, and why

Does anyone learn from the past?

Yes, many societies do see dangers in the ways in which they are acting. They regulate their agriculture and preserve their resources.

One developing country, in particular – Costa Rica in Central America – is widely admired for the way it looks after its natural habitats and plans its development carefully:

Costa Rican rainforest

- In the Environmental Performance Index, which measures countries on a wide range of environmental targets, Costa Rica is fifth. The first four are all small, wealthy European countries.
- Nature is not a free resource in Costa Rica; if you abuse it you pay.
- A quarter of the land is protected; a greater proportion than anywhere else in the world.
- The minister in charge of the environment decides about policies for mining and energy generation.
- Over 95% of Costa Rica's energy comes from hydro-electric and geo-thermal power – in other words, clean energy.
- A tax on carbon emissions is used to preserve its forests.
- The amount of forest in Costa Rica has doubled in 20 years.
- A tax on big water users is spent on keeping the rivers clean.

Find out more about Costa Rica. Compare the statistics above with those of your own country (or, if you are in Costa Rica, find out more about why you are a world leader).

Education for all

Unit question
What should a school look like?

Subject focus and objectives

Humanities
Skills (decision-making)
➔ Can you devise a strategy to deal with the problem of rural education, make a balanced judgement with conclusions, and decide on a course of action?

Language A
Style and language mechanics
➔ Can you use language in an entertaining manner to persuade students and their parents about the value of going to school?

Language B
Writing (message and organization/ language)
➔ Can you communicate information, ideas and opinions?

➔ Can you take part in formal exchanges related to international issues?

A rural school in Tanzania

Area of interaction
Community and service
➔ You will appreciate the difficulties involved in creating a community education centre, and the partnerships required to make it happen.

Approaches to learning focus
Thinking
➔ Using thinking skills to create a plan to build a community education centre in a village.

A Country Mouse invited a Town Mouse ... to pay him a visit, and partake of his country fare. As they were on the bare plough-lands, eating their wheat-stalks and roots pulled up from the hedge-row, the Town Mouse said to his friend: 'You live here the life of the ants, while in my house is the horn of plenty. I am surrounded with every luxury, and if you will come with me ... you shall have an ample share of my dainties.'

From Aesop's Fables
'*The Town Mouse and
The Country Mouse*'

agrarian • adjective •
Relating to agricultural or
rural matters.

Aesop's story above is often used to highlight the differences between rural and urban living and, although it goes on to feature some of the negative aspects of city-life, its message illustrates an unfortunate reality – the majority of the world's poorest people (those living on less than a dollar a day) live in rural areas, where farming is the main industry.

For those who live outside the mainstream education system, access to a good education is often limited. School attendance and school completion rates are low among these vulnerable groups, which often include girls, those from ethnic minorities, and those who live in the remotest areas (mountain regions and villages not accessible by road).

If the UN Millennium Development Goal of providing primary education for all is going to become a reality, the problem of educating rural populations must be addressed.

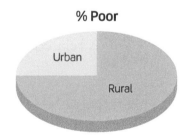

% Poor

Urban

Rural

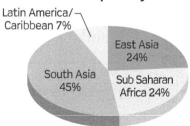

**Global distribution of
rural poverty**

Latin America/
Caribbean 7%

East Asia
24%

South Asia
45%

Sub Saharan
Africa 24%

Brainstorm

In this activity you will aim to answer the question:

Why are school attendance rates so low for poor, rural people?

Consider the following aspects of your own education and complete the 'You' column. Then think about how your answers might be different if you lived in a poor, rural village and complete that column.

Consideration	You	Rural villager	Priority
What do you eat for breakfast and lunch?			
Who pays for your schooling?			
How many hours do you work at your job outside of school?			
What level of education do the teachers at your school have?			
How many students are there in your class?			
How many water fountains/washrooms are there in your school?			
Are the things you are learning about relevant to your life and your future?			
Is the language you are instructed in the same as the one you speak at home?			
Is there a place where you could continue your education if you graduate?			

After completing the first two columns, the next step is to decide which of the considerations is the most important, and which are less so. This weighting technique helps organizations to decide about what to address urgently, and where to target their often-limited resources.

In your opinion, which of the above considerations are the most important and which are the least important? Complete the third column. Include an explanation if possible.

What is so important about an education?

Your parents have probably told you how important your education is more times than you care to remember! But have you ever asked yourself *why* it is so important?

You have probably heard something about needing an education 'so you can get a job'. But for many in the developing world, education is much more than the route to economic prosperity. As one of the most respected researchers into the effects of investing in education puts it:

> '*[education] is the key to scientific and technological advancement, the means to combat unemployment, the foundation of social equity, and the spread of political socialization and cultural vitality.*'

Education can also save lives. Studies show that for every year of primary education a girl receives, the survival rate of her children goes up by 10%!

Children working on the land in rural Burkina Faso

Think about some of the lofty outcomes outlined above. While some of them may be obvious, others might be less so. See if you can think of an explanation for how education can lead to:

a social equity

_____

_____

b cultural vitality

_____

_____

c reduced unemployment

_____

_____

d reduced infant mortality

_____

_____

(You might need to look up some of the terms used, such as: equity, vitality, and mortality.)

What makes a school a school?

In many ways, Madagascar is a model for the challenge of meeting the UN Millennium Development Goal of universal education. In 2001, less than two-thirds of Madagascan children were enrolled in school, and more than 85% of the mostly rural population lived on less than US$2 a day.

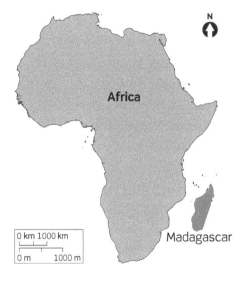

In this unit you will act as the education co-ordinator for a *commune rurale*, **a collection of remote villages or** *fokontanies* **in rural Madagascar. Your job is to put together a proposal to provide education for approximately 75 children.**

On page 33 you identified many of the general problems which help to keep rural children out of school. Now do some specific research about the situation in Madagascar. Go to the UN's Food and Agriculture Organization website, where you will find the photo story called 'A Malagasy Childhood' about a boy named Manisa from Ambohitseheno, a remote *fokontany* in Madagascar's central highlands:

http://www.fao.org/food/photo_report/madagascar/madagascar1_en.htm

Read about how Manisa's community is addressing the problem of hungry students by providing them with lunch from a school garden. Notice that school attendance is highest on the days when lunch is served.

1　Why do you think a school garden makes more sense for a poor, rural community than a traditional school lunch program?

_____

_____

_____

2　How would students' learning benefit if they are not hungry? (If you type "school breakfast" into a search engine you could access dozens of studies on the subject.)

_____

_____

_____

Our project plan

One of the biggest problems facing rural education is attracting good-quality teachers. Despite the fact that many countries have more teachers than they need in their cities, rural vacancies are still hard to fill. Surveys show that many teachers leave jobs in rural areas because of various forms of isolation – geographical, social, familial, cultural, and professional. The table on the right shows the ideas being used in some African countries to address this trend and encourage teachers to remain in rural areas.

Calling all teachers!

As a Madagascan education co-ordinator, create a recruitment poster in the second language, or Language B, that you are currently studying. Your aim is to attract teachers to the rural school you are planning. Besides finding candidates who can adjust to rural living, your 'ideal' teacher should be:

→ certified to teach more than one subject or grade level

→ able to teach students of a wide range of abilities in the same classroom

→ able to handle extracurricular activities, because most rural schools have very small staffs.

Think about how you could make your school and its rural area appealing. Madagascar might have an exotic or mysterious appeal to adventurous types. What are some of the iconic images you could use in your poster? Do some research about this island nation before you begin.

Your poster could use some of the ideas from the table, or others of your own invention. Make sure you provide references for any images you use. The text should be no more than 100 words.

Your teacher will provide you with the rubric that will be used to assess your poster.

Country	Incentive
Lesotho	A flat bonus is given to teachers prepared to teach in mountainous areas.
Malawi	The Government is considering offering housing, travel allowances, study leave, and teacher training opportunities for those who teach in rural areas.
Mozambique	Highly qualified rural teachers can receive bonuses of up to 100% of their salary.
Tanzania	Priority is given to housing for rural teachers
Uganda	A hardship allowance of 20% of their salary can be earned by those who teach in 'hard-to-reach' areas.

An exciting new technique is being used to get rural students back into the classroom in Madagascar. Four 15-minute radio programs have been created which are broadcast at various times of the week to help learners in remote communities. The Government has even bought more than 20,000 wind-up radios, so the message can be received in the homes and schools of villages without electricity. You can read more about this in the Press Centre section of the UNICEF website:

http://www.unicef.org/media/media_41408.html

The results have been very positive and the children love the characters, including animals like the Babakoto (lemur) who become their friends as they help to teach them literacy, numeracy, and important life-skills, including:

A Babakoto (Indri Indri) lemur in Madagascar

- ⇒ self-esteem
- ⇒ getting along with others
- ⇒ communication
- ⇒ gender equality
- ⇒ assessing risks
- ⇒ decision making
- ⇒ protecting the environment.

If you are going to be successful in getting the students in your area to come to the school you are building, you need to convince them, AND their parents, that school is important.

Calling all students!

Write an informative and entertaining radio play or short story about the importance of getting an education and attending school, which could be used in the next round of broadcasts. You could write it as a fable, like the Aesop's fable on page 32 – using Madagascan animals like the Babakoto. It is important for you to consider your tone and your audience. Stories with a purpose or a moral are fairly obvious in their message, but still have to hold the attention of the listener or reader.

Your teacher will provide you with the rubric that your short story will be assessed with.

More success stories

Fourth-grader Mino, is part of a 'big-sister' program started in Madagascar. She was chosen by her teacher to be a helper and friend to first-grade student Vololonirina, who was at risk of dropping out of school. Mino helps Vololonirina with her homework, picks her up on the way to school, plays with her at recess, and even advises her on hygiene and social skills. You can read more about them at the UNGEI (United Nations Girls' Education Initiative) website:

http://www.ungei.org/gapproject/madagascar_130.html

This program has been very successful and has had a surprising side effect – not only have little sisters been helped, but big-sisters have benefited as well.

1   Why do you think a program like this would help the 'big-sisters' as well as the 'little-sisters'?

_____

_____

_____

2   One of the conditions of joining the mentor program is that the 'big-sister' has to sign a contract. Do you think this step is necessary? Why/why not?

_____

_____

_____

3   Do you have a mentor program in your school? What skills or qualities could you bring to the program if you joined? If there is no mentor program at your school, what would be the value of starting one?

_____

_____

Forgotten children?

One of the things which is rarely considered is the plight of children who have been out of school for a while. Many might be too embarrassed to return to a classroom where they would be expected to learn with children much younger than themselves.

A unique program in Madagascar, based on the reading-for-all approach, is allowing students such as this to catch-up – with some learning the basics of reading in only a month of classes! An example from an English version of the program is shown on the right. You can read about how the program is helping at the UNESCO (United Nations Educational, Scientific and Cultural Organization) website:

www.unesco.org/en/education

Is this something your school might benefit from?

For many students, school is simply too far away to attend. Even if they were able to make the long round-trip on foot, there are other difficulties that await them there, as outlined in the table on page 33.

Some villages, NGOs, and even governments are recognizing that the traditional model of a school may not be working for these students.

'Decentralization' is a term being used more often when we talk about rural education. It means that the decision to build a school, hire the teachers, set the curriculum, the hours, and the language of instruction is in the hands of the parents and villagers themselves. In fact, in many places, the word 'school' has been replaced by 'community learning centre'.

7

I see the sun.
What is that?

What does Nat see in the sky near the sun?

An English example from the Reading for All Learners Programs, developed by Dr Alan Hofmeister in the USA (www.iseesam.com)

Building a school

As the education co-ordinator of the *commune rurale*, the village heads are looking to you to help them create a 'community learning centre' for 75 children. Your job is to tell them how to do this by answering the unit question:

What should a school look like?

Your teacher may decide to put you in a group with one or more other students for this project, since there are SO many things to consider. A lot of people are counting on you, so your report should be as thorough as possible. Use the research you have already completed, plus any further research you feel you need to do. You could use some, or all, of the questions in the table below as a guide, depending on where your interest and research takes you.

Your teacher will provide you with the rubric that your report will be assessed with.

The national flag of Madagascar

Money	Any plan needs a budget. What is the cost of building the school, paying the teachers, and purchasing the school's supplies?
Stakeholders	Who should be involved in the planning/building – villagers, NGOs, the Government, private investors, charities? How will you contact the right people to make this school happen? What will you ask them for?
Physical environment	What will the education centre look like? How many classrooms will you need? Where will your teachers stay? Will there be toilet facilities? Will you have electricity?
Running the school	How will you meet the needs of rural students? Will you be flexible around harvest/planting times, when students are needed at home? What subjects will you offer? What other programs will you offer to make sure that students stay in school?
Monitoring	How will you determine if your school is a success? How often will you check to see if your goals are being met? Which of the stakeholders will you need to report to?

Project evaluation

What I enjoyed about this unit, and why

What aspect I didn't enjoy, and why

What I did really well

What I did less well

What I would do differently next time

Which project work I liked best, and why

Prejudice and education

Almost 75% of Indians live in agricultural communities, and 80% (or 167 million) of these rural people are known as Dalits. If they had their own country, it would be the sixth largest, by population, in the world! Unfortunately, they have largely been excluded from playing their role in India's growing economy, because of prejudice. The United Nations defines caste as 'discrimination on the basis of work and descent', and India has tried to distance itself officially from the concept of the caste system by passing laws to protect Dalits – formerly known as 'untouchables'.

However, change has been slow coming and a 2006 study showed that:

- in 38% of villages Dalit children must sit separately in government schools
- most teachers are from a higher caste than the Dalit children, with many showing an open dislike of the Dalits and calling them 'forest people'
- in 70% of villages Dalit children cannot eat with other children
- in 48% of villages Dalit children are denied access to water sources
- Dalit children cannot drink from the same cup as other children
- 33% of health workers will not treat Dalit children
- bullying against Dalit children is not punished by many teachers
- 80% of Dalit children do not finish school.

Dalit schoolchildren with their teacher

There is an idea in education called the **hidden curriculum**. This is the unintended messages which are transmitted through everyday goings on in the school, rather than the formal learning in the timetable.

Discussion

If all the above bullet points were happening in a school, what would be the messages of that school's hidden curriculum? What changes would you make to deal with this?

4 Health and disease

Does an apple a day keep the doctor away?

Subject focus and objectives

Sciences
One world
↪ Can you appreciate that science is part of the world in which you live, and comment on ways in which science affects life, society and the world?

Communication in science
↪ Can you present information using a graphic organizer or poster, and also acknowledge your sources?

Physical education
Knowledge and understanding
↪ Can you describe and explain the basic principles that contribute to fitness and also their importance?

Area of interaction
Health and social education
↪ You will develop knowledge to make informed choices about your diet by studying the consequences of malnutrition.

Approaches to learning focus
Thinking
↪ Identifying problems, including deductive reasoning, and evaluating solutions to problems.

malnutrition • noun •
The impairment of physical
and/or mental health, as a
result of a failure to meet
nutritional requirements.

Malnutrition ...

Sudan. Ethiopia. Haiti. Images of malnutrition make it to our television screens when natural forces, unstable governments, and conflict come together to create famine. On these occasions, the United Nations (UN), individual governments, aid agencies, and the public at large, must unite to provide much needed emergency relief to prevent starvation and death.

A malnourished child in Sudan in 1994, with a vulture watching in the background

There is, however, a hidden face of malnutrition. Worldwide, up to two billion people manage to stay alive, but do not get enough to thrive. This hidden hunger is caused by a lack of essential vitamins and minerals (called micronutrients), and is often a result of low-calorie diets which are heavy in starchy foods but limited in meat, vegetables and fruits.

Making mud cookies in Haiti in 2007. Used to stave off hunger pains, the ingredients of the cookies are soil, salt and vegetable shortening.

The world sheds tears for the dead but not always for the survivors – and surviving is no simple task, considering that malnutrition is *the* biggest risk factor for illness worldwide. In fact, seven of the 13 leading risk factors associated with disease globally, including low body weight and deficiencies of zinc, iron and vitamin A, are associated with malnutrition. Some of the worst of these diseases/illnesses (HIV/AIDS, tuberculosis, diarrhea, and night blindness to name a few) all have links to poor nutrition.

Nowhere are these problems felt more deeply than in sub-Saharan Africa. This region is not only likely to miss targets set by the UN for hunger and disease reduction, but – in the case of hunger – conditions are actually getting worse. Over the last 30 years, food production in developing countries has tripled and the prices of staple crops, such as cereals, have dropped by almost 80%. However, these successes do not apply to sub-Saharan Africa, where overall food production per person is decreasing. Farmers make up the majority of Africa's hungry people, while at the same time generating the lowest quantity of food per hectare of any other place on Earth.

Our project plan

Adama's problems

Adama is a farmer from a village near Mopti in the Niger Delta of southern Mali. He has lost two of his seven children to malaria and one from diarrhea. Every year he plants millet – a tough grain – and every year his harvest is smaller than the year before. His remaining children are often hungry and sick. A worker from an aid agency told him that the soil he grows his crops in is slowly losing the nutrients they require to grow.

Last week, a man selling bags of fertilizer came to Adama's gate and promised that his fertilizer would increase Adama's crop by 300%. However, the price was more than he could afford. When he asked why it was so expensive, the man explained that in order to get the fertilizer from the seaport where he buys it, it had to be brought overland by car and then by bicycle – since there are no major roads leading to Adama's village. He would like to buy the fertilizer, especially if it will increase his harvest, help him to feed his family and keep them from getting sick, but he doesn't have enough money.

In some ways, Adama's problems are like the Russian nesting dolls on the right. At first it looks like a single problem – in this case sick children – but when you open it, you see that there are other problems inside which are partially responsible for the bigger problem. And once those problems are opened up, still more problems are found inside:

⇒ Disease (malaria/diarrhea)
⇒ The high price of fertilizer
⇒ Malnutrition
⇒ Soil depletion
⇒ Lack of roads
⇒ Cost of transport

1 Use the text about Adama and the bullet points above to label the dolls below with his problems. See if you can put them in an order where they connect from his biggest problem to more distant problems.

2 Explain which doll/problem you would focus your efforts on to help Adama most effectively.

The link between malnutrition and disease is described above as a direct link, but there are actually a number of steps connecting the two. As mentioned earlier, when micronutrients are in short supply, there can be dangerous consequences.

To investigate this, you could produce a graphic organizer like the one shown below – in this case representing the consequences of a zinc deficiency.

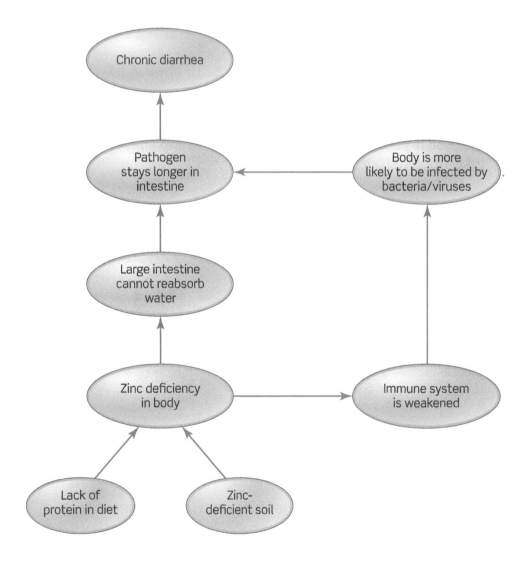

Similar to the nesting dolls example, a graphic organizer is a way of organizing collected information and displaying it in a way that enhances our understanding. For your own investigation, you could use either of these forms, OR design your own unique diagram.

Your investigation

Choose a micronutrient from the first table on the right to investigate, OR select one from your own research (as long as your teacher approves), OR you may want to start with a disease/illness that afflicts those in developing nations and work backwards to find a connection with a missing micronutrient (see the second table).

Your teacher may allow more than one person or group to choose the same micronutrient to investigate, as long as the endpoint (the illness) is different. For instance, there is a strong connection between zinc deficiency and HIV/AIDS, as well as with diarrhea.

Improving the diagram

You have probably noticed that the graphic organizer about the consequences of zinc deficiency seems incomplete. What could you add to your own diagram to make it more meaningful?

⇒ **Sources?**
A record of where you got your information from: textbook, website, journal, magazine. To achieve at the highest levels, you would indicate exactly which piece of information came from which source.

⇒ **Pictures?**
Sometimes adding photos or diagrams can enhance our understanding or grab our attention.

⇒ **Explanations?**
Graphic organizers are a great way to summarize and show links, but they sacrifice a bit of information. You could spell out the links more formally at the bottom of your diagram, or on a separate document.

Micronutrients
Folate
Iodine
Iron
Selenium
Vitamin A
Vitamin B$_{12}$
Vitamin C
Vitamin D
Vitamin K
Zinc

Diseases/afflictions
Anemia
Cretinism
Diarrhea
Goiter
HIV/AIDS
Keshan Disease
Night Blindness
Scurvy
Spina Bifida
Tuberculosis

➔ **Audience?**
You could simply submit the results of your investigation to your teacher, but you would probably learn a lot more if everyone shared their information with their classmates/other groups. How could you present this?

➔ **More information?**
Certainly your project will not be the first time that anyone has made the connection between missing nutrients and diseases. You will need to include what scientists, governments, and aid agencies are doing to address the problem (supplements? additives? engineered crops?) You might also explain how or why these micronutrients are missing in the first place from people's diets. Which foods would be a good source of the nutrient?

ISSUE LINK

You are likely to find that fertilizer is often recommended as a means of increasing food production and replenishing micronutrients (as with Adama's crops). The industrial process that creates fertilizer is intense and uses a tremendous amount of fossil fuels. Therefore, does the use of fertilizers really contribute to a green revolution?

Your teacher will provide you with the rubric to assess your performance.

A malnutrition breakthrough!

The girl in the photo is shown holding something called Plumpynut. It is the invention of a nutritionist at Medecins sans Frontieres – an organization which sends doctors to areas of conflict and famine. Plumpynut is being touted as a miracle cure for famine relief.

Do some research to find out the ingredients of Plumpynut, and why it has been so successful.

Is Plumpynut a sustainable way to provide nutrition?

How is your nutrition?

Complete a one-week inventory of everything you eat and drink. Wherever possible, you should attempt to define the size of the portion, because this has important implications for things like RDA (recommended daily allowance) and kcal (kilocalories – a measure of the energy content of your meal). You could use a table like the one below, or one that more closely matches your eating habits.

Day	Breakfast	Lunch	Supper	Snack
Monday	Grapefruit, Coffee (sugar/milk), Rye toast (butter)	Rice ($\frac{1}{2}$ cup), Aloo gobi, Dhal, Chicken leg (tikka masala), Diet Cola	Fish (steamed), Broccoli (oyster sauce), Tofu and mushroom (stir fry), Water	Peanuts ($\frac{1}{3}$ cup), Coffee (sugar/milk)
Tuesday				
Wednesday				
Thursday				
Friday				

Once your inventory is complete, you will need to analyze your data.

1 Work out your average daily caloric intake by finding out the number of calories in every item you have eaten and drank, and then dividing the total number of calories by the number of days covered by your survey. The caloric information can be found on packaging labels like the one on the right. For those students who eat only fresh foods, or who live in regions without food labels, you may have to rely on the values obtained from your own research to approximate your caloric intake.

    a Total number of calories consumed in the research period:

_____

_____

    b Average daily intake of calories:

_____

_____

_____

Serving Size: 1 entree

Amount per serving

Calories 175	Calories from fat 45

	% DV
Total Fat 5g	8%
Cholesterol 0mg	0%
Sodium 305mg	13%
Total Carbohydrate 30g	10%
Dietary Fiber 3g	12%
Protein 4g	8%

Unofficial Pts: 3

percent of Calories from
Fat – 25.7% **Carb** – 68.6% **Protein** – 9.1%
(Total may not equate to 100% due to rounding.)

2 Now work out the micronutrient content of your diet. This may be a bit more difficult than the macronutrients found above, so you may need to do some approximation. On the right is a table showing the minimum recommended daily levels of micronutrients in a person's diet. Try to work out what quantity of these nutrients you are receiving, based on your own diet inventory. Once this is complete, answer the following questions.

a Are you at risk of malnutrition?

_____

_____

b Should you be changing your diet?

_____

_____

Micronutrient	RDA
Vitamin A	5000 IU
Vitamin C	60 mg
Iron	18 mg
Vitamin D	400 IU
Vitamin E	30 IU
Vitamin K	80 µg
Thiamine	1.5 mg
Folate	400µg
Vitamin B_{12}	6.0 µg
Iodine	150µg
Zinc	15mg

Wrapping up

Assuming that receiving the proper micronutrients results in improved health and 'keeps the doctor away', use the information on the right (showing the micronutrients in a raw, unpeeled apple) to answer the unit question:

Does an apple a day keep the doctor away?

If your answer is that it could not keep the doctor away, is there another fruit or vegetable that could be substituted into the question above? Hint: You many want to look for things called 'superfoods'. Your teacher will provide you with the rubric to mark your inventory and responses to questions.

Nutrient (apple, raw, unpeeled)	Amounts per serving	% DV
Vitamin A	67.5 IU	1%
Vitamin C	5.7 mg	10%
Vitamin D	~	~
Vitamin E	0.2 mg	1%
Vitamin K	2.8 µg	3%
Folate	3.8 µg	1%
Vitamin B_{12}	0.0 µg	0%
Iron	0.1 mg	1%
Zinc	0.0 mg	0%
Selenium	0.0 µg	0%

_____

_____

_____

_____

_____

Project evaluation

What I enjoyed about this unit, and why

_____

_____

_____

What aspect I didn't enjoy, and why

_____

_____

_____

What I did really well

_____

_____

_____

What I did less well

_____

_____

_____

What I would do differently next time

_____

_____

_____

Which project work I liked best, and why

_____

_____

_____

Moving on

Malnutrition was defined earlier as not meeting somebody's nutritional requirements, which means that not getting enough food isn't the only way to be malnourished. So-called 'overnourishment' can be every bit as damaging to a person's health, and nowhere is this more obvious than in developed nations – where processed foods, a lack of portion control, and an overemphasis on meat in the diet is creating an army of sick individuals with the potential to bankrupt their countries' healthcare systems.

The Centre for Disease Control (CDC) has called the recent doubling in rates of Type 2, or adult-onset, diabetes an 'epidemic'. If current trends continue, one in three Americans will develop diabetes sometime in their lives – at the cost, on average, of 10-15 years of lifespan. Diabetes is the seventh leading cause of death in the USA, and the leading cause of adult blindness, kidney failure, and lower-limb amputations.

Perhaps the most troubling aspect is how the name itself – adult-onset diabetes – is becoming obsolete. Most developed nations have begun to report increasing numbers of adolescents (12-20 year olds) being diagnosed with Type 2 diabetes. In the past 20 years, Japan alone has seen cases of Type 2 diabetes in children increase by 30 times!

You should investigate how overnutrition and Type 2 diabetes are linked.

Unit question
How fair is a fair price?

Subject focus and objectives

Mathematics
Investigating patterns

⮞ Can you describe the relationship between cost and revenue, and supply and demand?

⮞ Can you use graphs and equations to solve problems?

Reflection in mathematics

⮞ Can you consider the reasonableness and importance of your findings regarding cost, revenue, and supply and demand curves?

Arts
Application

⮞ Can you articulate the idea of similarities and differences between farmers in developing and developed countries?

⮞ Can you develop the skills and apply the techniques of political cartoons to present this idea?

Area of interaction
Human ingenuity

⮞ You will appreciate the need for agricultural subsidies, and the consequences of these subsidies on developing nations and global commodity prices.

Approaches to learning focus
Communication

⮞ Selecting and organizing information, making connections between a variety of (primary and secondary sourced) resources.

Starting points

Agriculture has been around for more than ten thousand years, and so, it follows, have farmers. As Jonathan Swift suggests on the right, there may be no more important profession than producing the food that feeds us. There may also be no more difficult way of making a living, and this is reflected in the decline of farming in developed nations. The agricultural labour force decreased by 43% in the European Union between 1975 and 2000, and by 71% in Japan between 1965 and 2005. The US has lost almost 5 million farms since 1935 (on average one farm every two hours in 2008 alone).

To be fair, some of these decreases are probably due to changes in technology, but one thing that hasn't changed is the farmer's reliance on the natural world. They are bound to the regular rhythm of ploughing, sowing and reaping. With every spring planting comes sleepless nights, hoping the harvest will be plentiful. Trying to survive the cycles of boom and bust has always been a concern of farmers. In other industries, when times are tough, people stop doing what they are doing and find other employment.

'Whoever could make two ears of corn, or two blades of grass, to grow upon a spot of ground where only one grew before, would deserve better of mankind, and do more essential service to his country, than the whole race of politicians put together.'

Jonathan Swift, Gulliver's Travels, *first published in 1726*

Reflection

What would the consequences be if every time things were difficult farmers stopped farming and found other jobs?

_____

_____

_____

_____

A family farm in Arkansas, USA

Joseph Smith is a young farmer who lives outside Dumas, Arkansas in the USA. He farms over 5,000 acres with his father and sister, more than half of which are soybeans.

In this exercise you will investigate mathematically the costs and benefits of a typical American soybean farmer.

The table on the right shows the average costs of an American soybean farmer in 2006.

Item	Cost per acre ($US)
Seed	32.20
Fertilizer	13.05
Herbicide/ pesticide	14.46
Fuel, lube, electricity	13.51
Repairs	11.80
Other operating costs	8.29
Hired labour	1.78
Opportunity costs (land/ labour)	161.75
Taxes and crop insurance	7.93
Overhead	13.22
Total cost per acre	

1   Determine the farmer's total cost per acre and complete the table.

2   Express total cost in an equation: $y = m_1 x$ (m_1 is the cost per acre).

The average soybean farmer was able to produce 46 bushels per acre, with a market price of $5.54 per bushel in 2006.

3   Express total revenue using a similar equation to cost: $y = m_2x$ (m_2 is the revenue per acre).

4   Complete the table of values on the right for the two equations and determine the total cost (y_1) and total revenue (y_2) for the range of planted acres. *Ignore the final column at this stage (you will fill it in later).*

5   Graph this data using the blank graph below, or using a graphing calculator or Excel spreadsheet.

Acres planted (x)	Total cost (y₁)	Total revenue (y₂)	
0			
100			
200			
300			
400			
500			
600			
700			
800			
900			
1000			

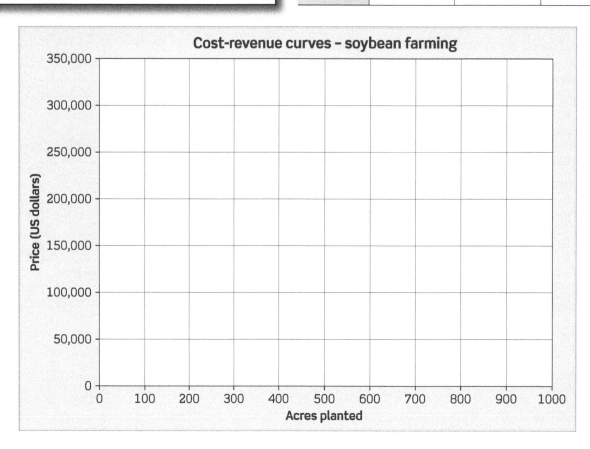

Cost-revenue curves – soybean farming

6   Outline any trends you can see in the data from the completed table and graph opposite.

_____

_____

7   The average acreage of soybeans planted in the USA in 2006 was 300. How much money (profit) would Joseph Smith make if he planted 300 acres of soybeans? Show your working.

_____

_____

8   How many acres of soybeans should be planted in order to maximize the profit from them?

_____

You have probably come to the conclusion that it is impossible to make money from farming soybeans. The US government also recognizes this, which is why it uses subsidies to help farmers. The latest US farm bill puts the guaranteed price of soybeans at $7 per bushel.

subsidy • noun • Economic benefit or financial aid provided by a government to maintain the income of the producers of critical or strategic products.

Your new total revenue equation would become:

$y = (\$7 \text{ per bushel} * 46 \text{ bushels per acre}) x$

or

$y = 322x$

9   Use the blank column in the table of values opposite to create a new set of y-coordinates for subsidized revenue. Then add in a new revenue curve on your graph to show subsidized revenue. Now go back and re-answer questions 6 to 8, based on this new revenue curve.

10   Discuss with a partner/classmate what a 'comfortable' or 'fair' living translates to in US dollars per year. Now use the revised data to work out how many acres of soybeans you would need to farm in order to achieve this goal. Is this a reasonable number?

You have probably figured out that making a profit in farming is difficult, even with subsidies. As you can see, the only way to 'succeed' is to scale up the size of your farm. Most family farmers do not have the money or the credit to purchase huge farms. Even though family farms are being lost at a staggering rate, the total amount of farmland has not decreased. Agribusinesses – also known as mega-farms – are corporations that buy up small farms and plant them 'fencerow to fencerow' with whatever commodity will provide them with the greatest profit. In fact, 74% of the billions in subsidies paid out in 2007 went to the top 10% of these mega-farms.

Subsidies may protect a few of the biggest farmers in developed countries, but flooding the market with too much of a commodity actually leads to lower prices, creating the need for more subsidies.

vicious circle • noun • A chain of events in which the response to one problem creates a new difficulty that makes the original problem worse.

Reflection

Does the model of subsidized farming in developed countries qualify as a vicious circle?

Subsidies are no small thing. In fact, every year developed countries pay between 300 and 400 billion US dollars to their farmers. The amount of support varies widely – with countries like New Zealand subsidizing less than 1% of farm costs and Switzerland up to 60%. You may be wondering how governments can afford these subsidies. In some cases, they pay farmers three or four times the market value of their crops!

Perspective

Imagine a place in the scenic mountains of Japan, where, between twice-daily massages and piped-in soothing music, you are fed the finest imported foods and ice-cold beer. What you are picturing is not a luxury spa but the daily routine of Wagyu cattle. These are used to produce the world's most expensive meat – Kobe beef – which can fetch prices of US$600 a kilogram. What's interesting is that each cow receives the equivalent of US$7 a day in subsidies from the Japanese government. This is more than the daily wage of half the world's population!

Reflection

1   Where do governments get the billions of dollars they pay in subsidies to farmers? You may need to do some research.

_____

_____

_____

_____

2   Most of the countries in the developed world contribute development assistance or 'Aid' (blue bars) to developing nations. How do the agricultural subsidies they pay to their own farmers (red bars) compare?

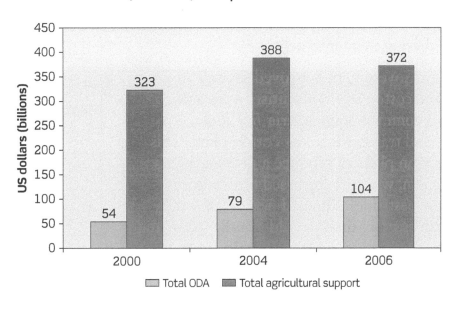

3   How do you think this affects a farmer in the developing world trying to sell his or her crop on the 'open' market?

_____

_____

_____

_____

A cotton farm in Guntur, India

Under the shadowy skies of a delayed monsoon, a farmer borrows the money for a bottle of pesticide. It is not going to be used on his two acres of cotton, which have long been overrun with bollworms. Instead, the farmer intends to drink the poison – joining the approximately 200,000 farmers in India who have committed suicide since 1997.

One of the problems with growing cotton is the many pests capable of destroying the crop – especially the bollworm, which burrows into the cotton boll and feeds on its contents, causing it to rot. One of the ways to control this pest is to use pesticides. Despite covering less than 5% of India's farmland, cotton accounts for 55% of the nation's pesticide use! However, as pests become resistant to the poison, farmers are forced to spray more often (sometimes dozens of times), driving them into debt.

In 2002, the Indian Government approved the sale of genetically modified cotton seeds. Scientists were able to take a gene from a common soil bacteria *Bacillus thuringiensis* (Bt) and transfer it to the cotton plant. This gene allows the cotton plant to produce a protein that is toxic to the bollworm, which is supposed to drastically reduce the need for pesticides. The bad news is that the seeds cost many times more than the old non-Bt seeds, and, more importantly, they do not do as well in dry conditions. Very few farmers in India's cotton belt have any irrigation, so they rely on the monsoon rains. If the rains are delayed, light, or too heavy, the Bt seeds give almost no benefits.

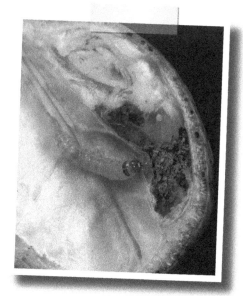

A bollworm inside a cotton boll, causing it to rot

1   There are a number of mathematical concepts contained in the paragraphs above. See if you can identify or highlight instances of:

    a   probability _____

    b   statistics _____

    c   cost-benefit _____

    d   ratio _____

Many of the problems facing India's cotton farmers would disappear if the price of cotton were higher. As journalist Jaideep Hardikar points out: 'India's cotton farmers could easily compete at a price of 3,500 rupees a bushel. Today they usually get less than 2,000 rupees (below the cost of production), and it is impossible to make even 10,000 rupees a year from an eight-hectare plot. That is just US$200 for an entire family to live on.'

Many people argue that subsidies harm farmers in developing nations by rewarding farmers in developed nations for overproducing commodities – which in turn drives down the world price.

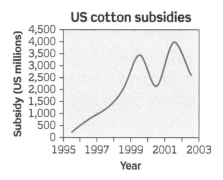

2 For each of the graphs on the right:

a Draw on the line of best fit (trend line).

b Work out the equation of the line in the form y = mx+b and add it underneath.

c Investigate whether there is evidence of a correlation between any of the equations/graphs.

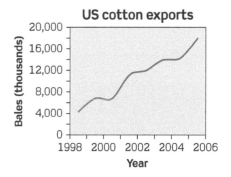

3 Use your answers from above to determine whether the prices of subsidized commodities are FAIR. Remember the unit question:

How fair is a fair price?

Your teacher will provide you with the rubric for assessing your work.

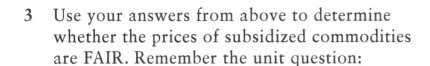

Every picture tells a story

Political pictures have been around since the early 1500s, when visual propaganda was used to promote the religious Reformation in Europe. Pictures can be used to summarize the essence of a problem or issue, as well as delivering the artist's particular feeling or opinion on the matter.

'The Silent Wave', drawn by the artist Alfredo Sabat in 2005

1 Take a look at the picture on the right and then answer as many of the following questions as possible.

   a What event or idea is the picture referring to?

   b What symbols (if any) are contained in the picture, and what purpose do they serve?

   c Is the picture realistic or are there distorted/exaggerated characters and symbols?

   d Is the artist trying to persuade the reader? Are the artist's beliefs or opinions evident?

2 Draw your own political picture. The theme should be based around the unit question:

How fair is a fair price?

There are a number of smaller ideas contained in this unit that may inspire you (see the bullets on the right). Your teacher will provide you with the rubric for the assessment of this piece.

⇒ The disparity between farmers in developing and developed nations

⇒ The similar difficulties shared by farmers in developed and developing nations

⇒ The impact of subsidies on either or both

⇒ Farmer suicides

⇒ Genetically engineered crops

⇒ Loss of family farms and growth of agribusiness

⇒ Growing costs of materials (seed, pesticide) vs. shrinking revenues

You could also draw a second political picture about any other subject in this book which has made you feel strongly.

Project evaluation

What I enjoyed about this unit, and why

_____

_____

_____

What aspect I didn't enjoy, and why

_____

_____

_____

What I did really well

_____

_____

_____

What I did less well

_____

_____

_____

What I would do differently next time

_____

_____

_____

Which project work I liked best, and why

_____

_____

_____

Fairtrade is a growing social movement that uses a market approach to help farmers in developing countries get a 'fair' price for a variety of goods, including bananas, chocolate, cocoa, coffee, cotton, sugar, and tea.

As you can see in the graph on the right, the movement has been steadily growing, directly benefitting, according to some estimates, 7.5 million people.

Sales of fairtrade-certified goods have grown steadily by almost 50% from year to year, with sales reaching US$3.2 billion worldwide in 2007.

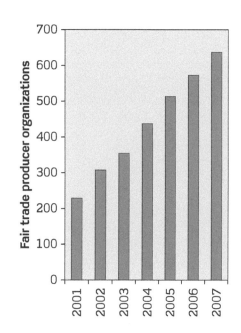

The fairtrade model works under the following principles:

- Prices that cover sustainable production – even when world market prices are low.
- A fairtrade premium, paid on top of the agreed price, which can be invested in healthcare, education, or improvements in farming or processing.
- Partnerships that give producers a voice in managing their crop, including standards, prices, and overall strategy.

Visit the FLO (Fairtrade Labelling Organizations International) website and investigate what it means to have sustainable production. You will see that it is no easy task to meet the high standards insisted upon if a farmer is going to be fairtrade certified.

Ask yourself if the Arkansas soybean farmer, the agribusiness mega-farm, or the Indian cotton farmer would have a chance of qualifying as a fairtrade business.

6 Environmental sustainability

Unit question
How green are green fuels?

Subject focus and objectives

Sciences
Scientific enquiry
⇢ Can you design an investigation that reflects one aspect of the green fuel debate, including variables and controls, and comment on the method and accuracy of the results?

Data processing
⇢ Can you organize, transform, present, and analyze collected data, and make a simple conclusion?

Humanities
Concepts – systems
⇢ Can you identify and understand how business and agriculture systems operate?

Decision-making skills
⇢ Can you formulate arguments, make considered judgements and draw basic conclusions about green fuels?

Area of interaction
Environments
⇢ You will try to understand and evaluate the issue of biofuels and their impacts on other systems.

Approaches to learning focus
Transfer
⇢ Inquiring in different contexts, including changing the context of an inquiry to gain various perspectives.

The United Nations Millennium Development Goal for environmental sustainability calls for, among other things, a 'significant' reduction in carbon dioxide (CO_2) emissions. In Project Organizer 1, Unit 6, the connection was made between fossil fuel combustion, rising CO_2 emissions, and global climate change. One of the methods now being suggested to reduce CO_2 emissions is the use of alternative fuels or biofuels – the most common of which is ethanol.

panacea • noun • An answer or solution for all problems or difficulties.

The theory behind biofuels is shown in the diagram. When plants grow, they take in CO_2 as part of the process of photosynthesis and store it as chemical energy. In the case of corn, this storage is mostly as starch. When the corn is harvested and sent to a processing plant, it is ground and separated into sugars – using special chemicals called enzymes. The sugars are then fermented using yeast and a product of this reaction – ethanol – is distilled for use as fuel. Burning this fuel releases the CO_2 back into the atmosphere. This perfect cycle results in no 'new' CO_2 entering the atmosphere – unlike the burning of fossil fuels such as gasoline, diesel, and natural gas. Using this model, it is clear why ethanol made from corn and other crops is considered to be a 'green' fuel.

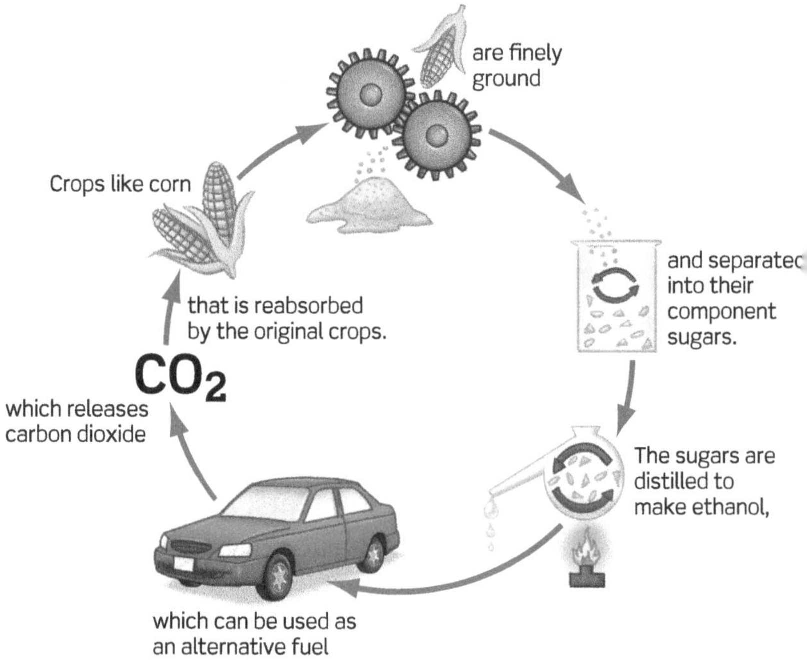

are finely ground

Crops like corn

that is reabsorbed by the original crops.

CO2

which releases carbon dioxide

which can be used as an alternative fuel

and separated into their component sugars.

The sugars are distilled to make ethanol,

Unfortunately, there is more to the picture above than is shown in the diagram. Do some Internet research on the subject of biofuels. Try to familiarize yourself with the issues and pay special attention to some of the pros and cons being discussed. Keep an eye on **bias** (would the pros/cons list look the same at treehugger.com as it would at economist.com?).

Fill in the table on the right with the results of your research. You will use this later to help you come up with an answer to the unit question:

How green are green fuels?

You could make your pros and cons list more valuable by using some simple organizing techniques, and by adding further information.

One such technique would be to RANK both sides of your list – best to worst, most impact to least impact, most helpful to least helpful. This will force you to think about which of the points are really important, and *why* they are important. You could even create a separate table with extra columns to include these ranks and your reasons for them.

You could also go through the table and look for concepts and terms that you are unfamiliar with and then explain/define them. It would be difficult for you to assign a rank to a point about, for example, eutrophication if you didn't know what it was.

Before you decide which side of the fence you are on when it comes to biofuels, you should investigate some of the pros and cons yourself. On the next three pages are four suggestions for experiments. Two of them are laid out in greater detail, while the other two are more open. You and/or your classmates could try different experiments and then report the results to each other. This will of course depend on the availability of materials. Your teacher will provide you with the rubrics used to assess your experiments and write-ups.

PROS	CONS

Experiment A – fermentation

A microorganism called yeast is used to convert corn into ethanol. The chemical reaction – called fermentation – that produces ethanol is:

$$\text{carbohydrate} \xrightarrow{\text{yeast}} \text{carbon dioxide} + \text{ethanol}$$

Starch is not the best 'fuel' for yeast to work with. It must first be broken down into smaller sugars that yeast can use. Some other crops store their chemical energy in forms which yeast prefers. You might like to design an experiment to investigate which carbohydrate produces the most ethanol – as evidence of which one yeast likes best.

Beets and sugar cane are two common alternatives to corn. If you have a juicer, you could create carb-rich liquids from various fruits/vegetables/grasses and test which produces the most ethanol. Corn starch suspended in water could be used as a 'standard' for comparison. A typical recipe for 'activating' yeast would be 5g of table sugar (sucrose) to a cup of *warm* water and a packet of yeast. This may help you to design a fair test using different juices.

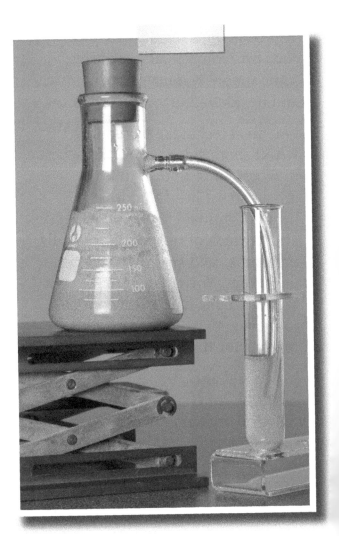

Fermentation in action

Although it will smell, the ethanol will not present itself as an easily measured quantity. Instead, it will be mixed in with a sticky brown mixture of water, carbohydrate and yeast. However, if you look at the equation above, you will see that the *other* bi-product of the reaction is carbon dioxide (CO_2). Measuring CO_2 would be an easy way to estimate how much ethanol has been produced.

A gas could be detected in several ways:

⇒ When CO_2 is produced, the gas will begin to fill the container. If the container is corked, the pressure inside will increase. Do you have a way of measuring the pressure inside the container? Would a balloon over the opening or a pressure sensor work?

⇒ When CO_2 is produced, it mixes with water and makes a weak acid called carbonic acid. The more CO_2 that is produced, the more acidic the solution becomes. Do you have a way of measuring the pH of a solution?

⇒ Any gas produced in a liquid medium, like your yeast experiment, will produce bubbles. If more bubbles of gas are produced, more ethanol is produced as well. Do you have a way of measuring the height of the bubbles?

Experiment B – eutrophication

When excess nutrients from over-fertilized crops like corn make their way into waterways, the results can be devastating. Aquatic plants, like algae, grow so fast with these excess nutrients that they blanket out the sun for organisms deeper in the water. Then, when the algae dies, bacteria decompose it and use up all of the oxygen in the water – killing everything that can't move away. Every year a dead zone the size of the state of New Jersey is created in the Gulf of Mexico – mostly because of the agricultural runoff from Midwest farms that drain into the Mississippi River Basin.

An outbreak of algae off the coast of Qingdao in China - the host city for the 2008 Olympic Games sailing events

Design an experiment to measure the effect of agricultural runoff (maybe you could use liquid fertilizer from a plant store) on some common aquatic plants, like algae or duckweed. Both plants could be purchased from a science supplier, or perhaps a store that sells aquarium supplies. Alternatively, you could 'harvest' some from a local pond or waterway and cultivate it in class so that there is enough for everyone to get started.

You might want to consider the following questions:

1 How could you use the fertilizer to create different conditions in different containers?
2 How will you make sure that you have added the same number of plants/algae to each of your different containers?
3 What other conditions should you have in your containers that will help with plant growth?
4 What will you need to keep the same (*controlled*) in the containers to make sure that your test is fair?
5 How will you measure how much or how fast the plants/algae are growing?
6 How long should you let the experiment run for?

Two other experiments

Fertilizer – Design an experiment to see how fertilizer affects the growth of plants. You may have already done a similar experiment in your science career. You could check with your teacher for help with designing this experiment.

Runoff – How much of the fertilizer that we put on crops is absorbed, and how much makes its way into runoff? Design an experiment to test the levels of nutrients (nitrogen, phosphorous, etc.):

⇒ in a container of water plus fertilizer before watering plants,

⇒ and then again in the water that seeps through the soil and into a collecting device after the plants have been watered/fertilized.

The three sisters

No matter how 'green' you decide ethanol is, one thing is certain – corn has changed significantly since its early cultivation by Native Americans (see right). The 'three sisters' system was a marvel of agricultural ingenuity. The corn provided a stalk for the beans to grow up, while the beans returned valuable nitrogen to the soil. The leaves of the squash created ground cover, which helped to collect and hold water and prevented the growth of weeds. All of this has now been replaced with modern farming techniques that are designed to grow the most corn possible on the smallest plots of land.

'In late spring, we plant the corn and beans and squash. They're not just plants – we call them the three sisters. We plant them together, three kinds of seeds in one hole. They want to be together with each other, just as we Indians want to be together with each other. So long as the three sisters are with us, we know that we will never starve. The Creator sends them to us each year. We celebrate them now. We thank Him for the gift He gives us today and every day.'

Iroquois Chief Louis Farmer (Onondaga Nation)

Try to match the facts below about modern corn with the 'three sisters' approach above. Include a brief reflection about which method you prefer.

a   In 2008, more than 80% of the corn grown in the USA was from genetically modified seed, which had been engineered to resist pests and withstand large doses of herbicide.

Three sisters: _____

_____

b   Corn requires huge amounts of nitrogen-based fertilizer, at a cost of $93US per acre – the highest of any crop – accounting for 40% of a farmer's operating budget (planting, growing, and harvesting).

Three sisters: _____

_____

Not only has the growing of corn changed, but its uses have evolved as well. Referring to North Americans, Michael Pollan points out in *The Omnivore's Dilemma*:

> 'You are what you eat it's often said, and if this is true, then what we mostly are is … processed corn'.

Since most livestock are fed with corn, you could correctly say when you eat a piece of meat that you are actually eating corn (along with the milk, cheese, and yoghurt made from the animal's milk).

With processed foods, following the trail of corn becomes more difficult – as in the following paragraph from *The Omnivore's Dilemma*:

> 'Head over to the processed foods and you find ever more intricate manifestations of corn. A chicken nugget, for example, piles corn upon corn: what chicken it contains consists of corn, of course, but so do most of its other constituents, including the modified corn starch that glues the thing together, the corn flour in the batter that coats it, and the corn oil in which it gets fried … even the citric acid that keeps the nugget "fresh" … [is] derived from corn.'

High fructose corn syrup is the number one sweetener in the USA and is found in everything from sodas and juices to less-obvious items like breads, condiments and soups. Many of the strange and unpronounceable ingredients found on processed food labels – maltodextrin, lecithin, dextrose, xanthan gum – are also derivatives of corn. In fact, of the 45,000 or so products on offer in a typical American supermarket, more than 25% of them contain corn. If so much of what Americans eat depends on corn, how will an increasing demand for ethanol affect that?

DID YOU KNOW?

Filling an SUV with one tank of ethanol requires as much as 450 pounds of corn. Enough to feed a person for a year!

The four graphs below have been provided to see if you can make a connection between ethanol production, food prices, and their impact on the world's poorest peoples. Write a brief description of what you think each graph illustrates. Once this is complete, try to write a paragraph that links all four of the graphs together. In your paragraph you should include a prediction of what you think will happen if the demand for ethanol continues to increase.

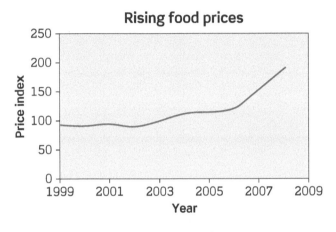

Explanation:

_____

_____

_____

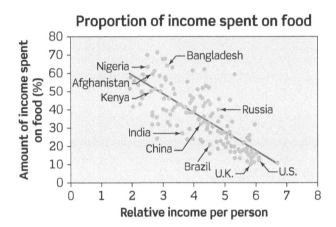

Explanation:

_____

_____

_____

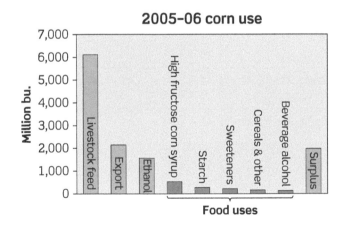

Explanation:

_____

_____

_____

Corn used in ethanol production, 1980–2008

Explanation:

_____

_____

_____

Paragraph:

_____

_____

_____

_____

_____

_____

_____

Wrapping up

You have been asked to work on the President's Special Advisory Committee on Biofuels. The President now has to decide whether or not to continue with the past Administration's decision to pursue ethanol as a fuel source. Your committee has been asked to evaluate the impact of green fuels. You must answer the question set at the beginning of this unit:

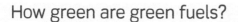

How green are green fuels?

Write a 'brief' of your findings. The President values your opinion and considers you to be an expert. Therefore, in your brief, you must make your position clear, while giving him all the relevant information he needs to decide whether or not he agrees with you. This means that your approach needs to be balanced. If you decide that biofuels like ethanol are 'green', you must still present the other side of the argument, and vice versa if you decide they are not.

Your teacher will provide you with the rubric for this assignment and will be looking for your ability to examine how systems (the government, agriculture, the environment) are connected, and also your ability to make a decision about a complicated issue.

Project evaluation

What I enjoyed about this unit, and why

_____

_____

_____

What aspect I didn't enjoy, and why

_____

_____

_____

What I did really well

_____

_____

_____

What I did less well

_____

_____

_____

What I would do differently next time

_____

_____

_____

Which project work I liked best, and why

_____

_____

_____

Grass-oline?

Switchgrass is a perennial grass native to prairie ecosystems. It can reach heights of more than two metres, and grows extremely quickly on marginal land – soil not fit for planting crops. This growth can be achieved largely without the use of pesticides and herbicides, and very little (if any) fertilizer is required. When the grass is cut, dried, and formed into pellets, it burns very efficiently and can be used directly to power furnaces and heat buildings. In fact, for every kcal of energy input used to grow switchgrass – harvesting, watering, fertilizing, etc. – the output is 11kcal. This is an amazing return on the investment.

> **perennial** • adjective •
> Persisting for several years, usually with new growth.

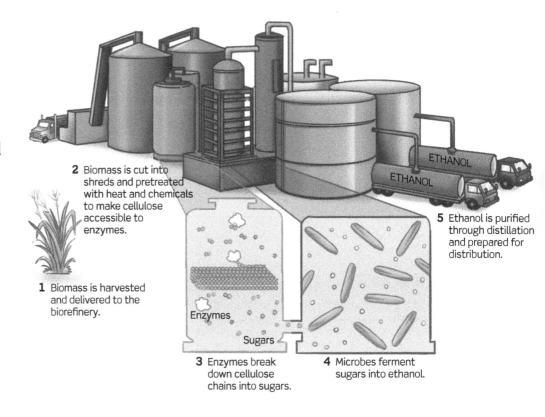

1 Biomass is harvested and delivered to the biorefinery.

2 Biomass is cut into shreds and pretreated with heat and chemicals to make cellulose accessible to enzymes.

3 Enzymes break down cellulose chains into sugars.

4 Microbes ferment sugars into ethanol.

5 Ethanol is purified through distillation and prepared for distribution.

Enzymes

Sugars

ETHANOL

ETHANOL

This is important, because the fossil fuels currently used to heat buildings in northern climates generate even more greenhouse gases than are generated by transportation. Unfortunately, we have a reliance on *liquid* fuels. The cellulose in switchgrass – the special carbohydrate that makes cell walls so rigid – can be converted into liquid using much the same method as the conversion of cornstarch into ethanol. However, some of the same problems with the conversion process that you discovered earlier in your research will still apply.

Should we reconsider what form our fuel should take?

Acknowledgments

The publisher would like to thank the following for permission to reproduce photographs:

Cover photo Phi2/iStock; Corel; **P7** Altrendo/Getty Images; **P8** Win Initiative/Getty Images; **P10t** Yawar Nazir/Getty Images, **P10b** AFP/Getty Images; **P18** Getty Images; **P19** Modestlife/Shutterstock; **P20** Wolfgang Kaehler/Alamy; **P21** National Geographic/Getty Images; **P23t** Gary Yim/Shutterstock, **P23b** Jenny Matthews/Alamy; **P24b** Getty Images News; **P24t** Chris Howes/Wild Places Photography; **P27** Gavin Hellier/Alamy; **P30** Bill Bachmann/Alamy; **P31** M J Photography/Alamy; **P32** Chris Beetles Gallery/Bridgeman Art Gallery; **P34** Mark Edwards/Still Pictures; **P37** John Warburton-Lee/Photolibrary; **P38** Stuart Fox/Getty Images; **P39** Dr Alan Hofmeister/Learning for all Readers; **P43** Viktar Malyshchyts; **P44** Kevin Carter/ Megan Patricia Carter Trust/Sygma/Corbis; **P45** Ariana Cubillos/Press Association; **P46** Michael Dwyer/Alamy; **P47** IntraClique,LLC/Shutterstock; **P50** Andrew Aitchison/Alamy; **P55** Lou Beach; **P56** Farmers Feed Cities; **P57** Kirk Edwards/ Photolibrary; **P62** Chris Cattlin/Frank Lane Picture Agency; **P64** Alfredo Sabat; **P66** Steven May/Alamy; **P67** James Steidl/Shutterstock; **P70** Martyn Chillmaid; **P71** Associated Press/ Press Association; **P73** Marilyn Angel Wynn/Nativestock.com/Getty Images; **P74** Arni Katz/ Alamy; **P76** Time & Life Pictures/Getty Images.

Illustrations are by: **P54** Paul Daviz; other illustrations are by Q2A Media.